I am a Kid... One of a Kind!

Bilingual book

English/Spanish

By
Ken Stevens

Illustrated by
Carmen Pacheco

Balboa Press books may be ordered through booksellers or by contacting:

Balboa Press
A Division of Hay House
1663 Liberty Drive
Bloomington, IN 47403
www.balboapress.com
844-682-1282

Because of the dynamic nature of the Internet, any web addresses or links contained in this book may have changed since publication and may no longer be valid. The views expressed in this work are solely those of the author and do not necessarily reflect the views of the publisher, and the publisher hereby disclaims any responsibility for them.

ISBN: 979-8-7652-2520-2 (sc)
ISBN: 979-8-7652-2521-9 (e)

Library of Congress Control Number: 2022903193

Print information available on the last page.

Balboa Press rev. date: 04/21/2022

I am a Kid...
One
of a Kind!

By Ken Stevens
Illustrated by Carmen Pacheco

This book is dedicated to each person's unique personality. Helping young and old kids to embrace the virtues freely available to enjoy each day. In any language we are each very special and loved.

Why am I?
Because... I am.

Love showed up
and I was created.

Draw or paste a picture of
you in the heart of the plant.

Why am I here?
I showed up
to be me...

...One of a kind.

Use this space to trace, stamp or paint your one-of-a-kind hand.

5

Why am I alive?
When I breathe
in and out, my heart
shows up and beats.

Feel your heart beating.

Draw a picture of your heart
and write "Thank you"

Why am I thinking?
My brain shows up
each day.

Thinking helps us
to enjoy life.

Think of two good thoughts
and share them with another
or draw a picture of them in
the bubbles.

Why am I funny?
I show up funny when I say silly things.

Say something silly and see the Penguins laugh

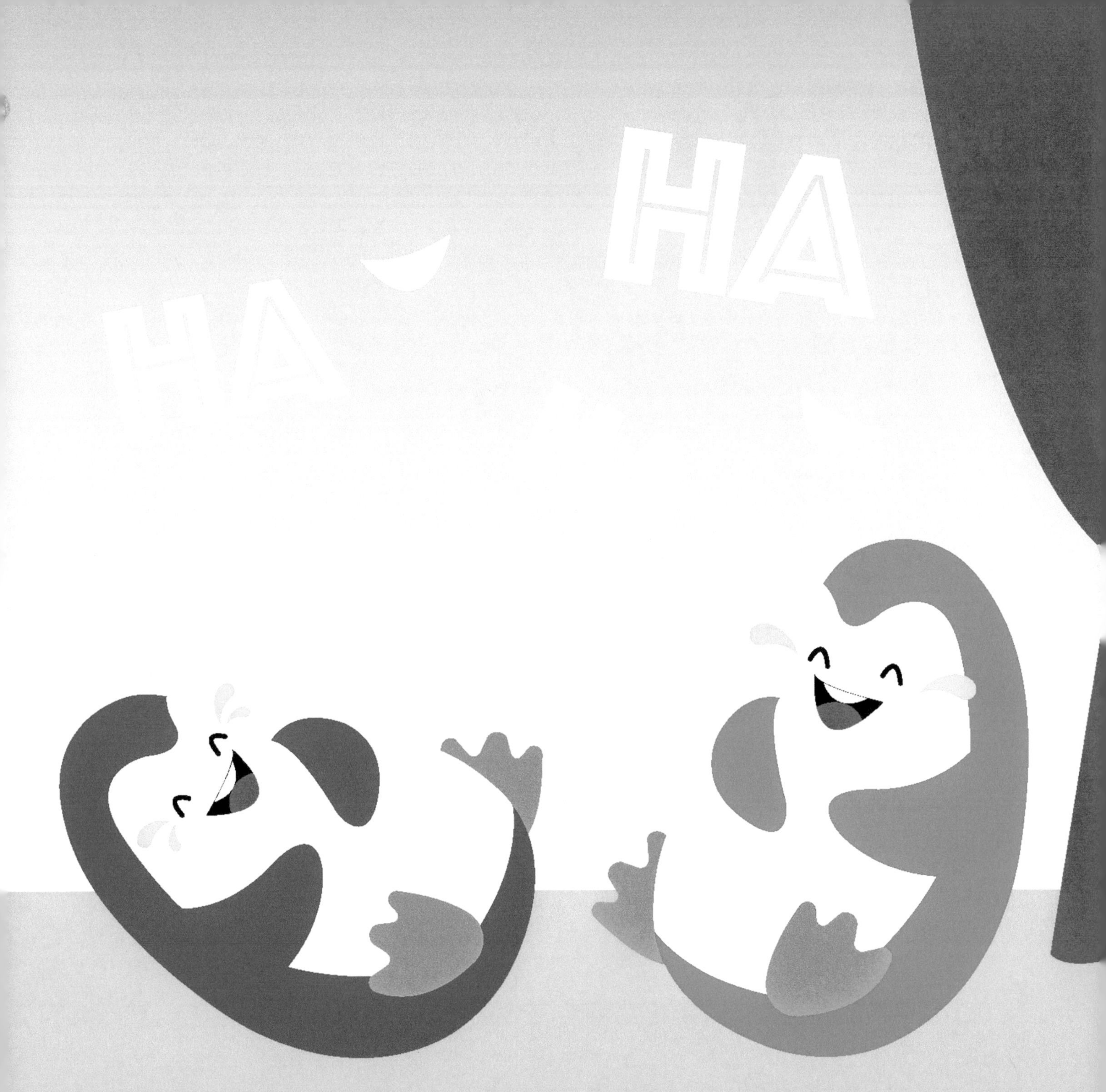
HA
HA

**Why am I smart?
I show up smart when
I learn new things
like good manners
and respecting others.**

Think of three new things
you learned today.

Why am I smiling?

Showing up with a smile makes me and others feel good.

Share a smile. Did it make you feel good? Did it make someone else smile too?

Why am I kind?
Showing up kind
shares my love
with others.

**Sharing is caring
and kind too.**

Draw or pick a flower and give it to someone you care about.

Why am I gentle?

Showing up gentle
lets others know
I care.

Draw or pick a flower and give it to someone you care about.

Why am I gentle?

Showing up gentle
lets others know
I care.

Touch your left hand with your right finger as gentle as you can. Did it feel soft? Whisper. Show up with a gentle voice.

Why am I happy?

Showing up happy is my gift to the world.

Draw a picture of the world with a big smile. Draw a picture of you smiling on top of the world.
Add all your friends and family too.

Why am I loved?

When I show up with love it comes back to me.

Hug someone for 2 seconds.
Hug someone for 7 seconds.
Did you feel more love
the second time?

Hugs

23

Why am I safe?
When I show up
"feeling" safe...
I am safe.

Hold your mom or dad's or
friend's hand. Do you "feel" safe?
Hold hands when you go places,
it will help you feel safe and loved.
At night, "feel" safe by being
tucked in bed.

Why am I sleepy?

Each day we do our best. I show up sleepy now to get some rest.

Put your hand close to your mouth and yawn. Did it make you feel sleepy? Give kisses good night and close your eyes gently to sleep.

Soy especial

libro bilingue

Ingles/Español

Autor
Ken Stevens

Illustrado por
Carmen Pacheco

¿Por qué estoy aquí?
Porque aquí estoy.

El amor apareció y fui creado.

Dibuja o pega una foto tuya en el corazón de la planta.

¿Por qué existo?
Existo para ser yo...

...alguien especial.

Usa este espacio para dibujar, pintar o estampar una mano única.

33

¿Por qué vivo?

Cuando respiro,
mi corazón dice
presente y late.

Siente tu corazón latir.
Haz un dibujo de tu corazón
y escribe "Gracias".

¿Por qué pienso?

Porque mi cerebro está activo cada día.

Pensar nos ayuda a disfrutar la vida.

Piensa en dos pensamientos y compártelos con alguien o dibújalos en las burbujas.

¿Por qué soy gracioso?

Soy gracioso cuando cuento chistes.

Cuenta un chiste y ve como los pingüinos ríen.

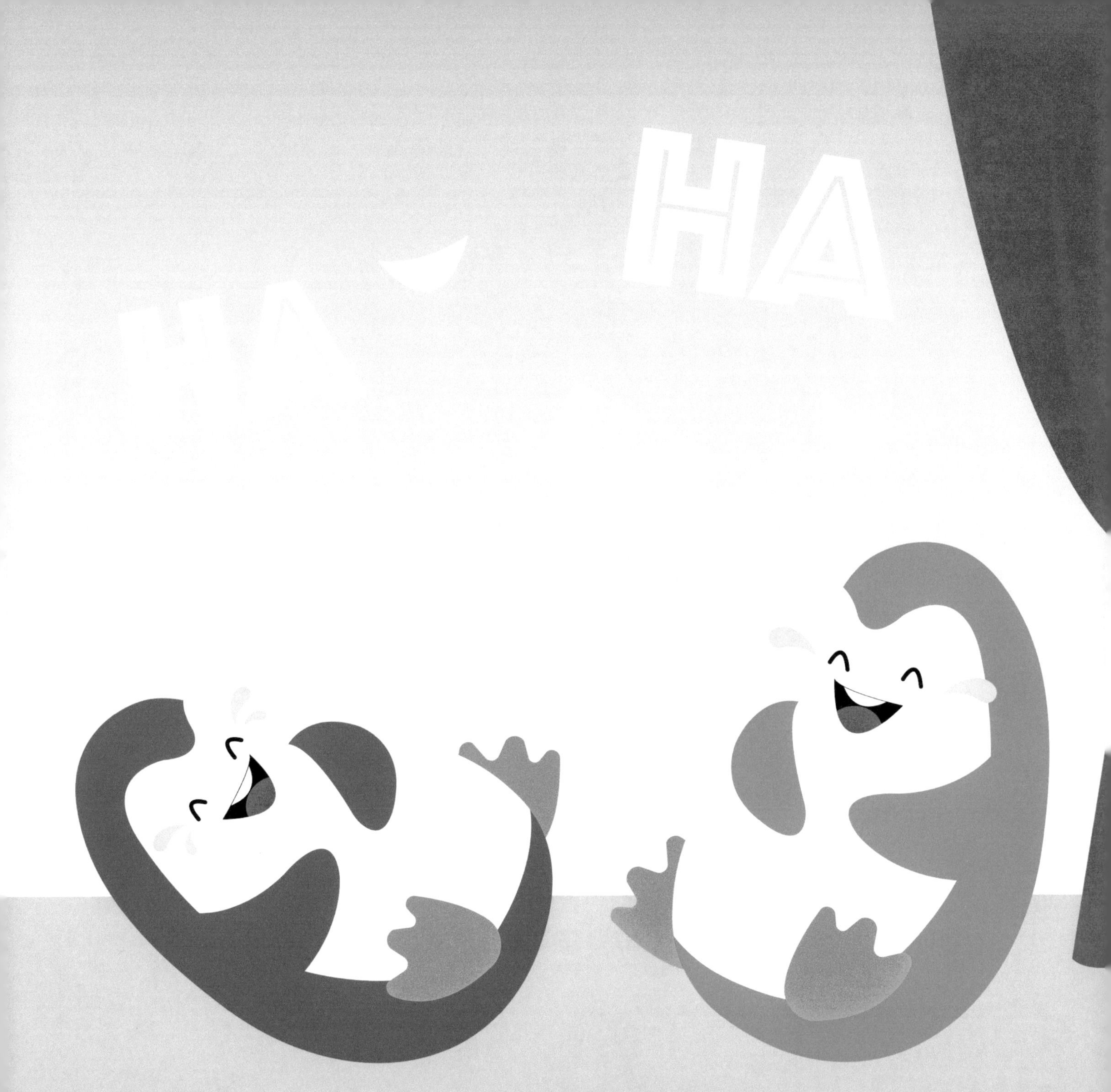
HA
HA

¿Por qué soy inteligente?

Soy inteligente porque aprendo cosas nuevas como buenos modales y respetar a los demás.

Piensa en tres cosas nuevas que aprendiste hoy.

¿Por qué sonrío?

Mostrar una sonrisa me hace sentir bien a mí y a los demás.

Comparte una sonrisa.
¿Te hizo sentir bien? ¿Hizo que alguien más sonriera también?

¿Por qué soy amable?

Mostrarme amable comparte mi amor con los demás.

Compartir es demostrar interés y ser amable también.

Dibuja o recoge una flor y dásela a alguien que te importe.

¿Por qué soy tierno?

Mostrarse gentil les permite a los demás saber que me importan.

Toca tu mano
izquierda con tu
dedo derecho tan
suavemente como
puedas. ¿Se sintió
suave?

Susurra. Preséntate
con una voz tierna
y gentil.

¿Por qué estoy feliz?
Mostrarme feliz es
mi regalo para el mundo.

Haz un dibujo del mundo con una gran sonrisa. Haz un dibujo de ti sonriendo en la cima del mundo. Incluye a todos tus amigos y familiares también.

¿Por qué soy amado?

Cuando muestro amor, vuelve a mí.

Abraza a alguien por 2 segundos. Abraza a alguien durante 7 segundos. ¿Sentiste más amor la segunda vez?

Abrazos

51

¿Por qué me siento a salvo?

Cuando me siento seguro me siento a salvo.

Toma la mano de tu mamá, papá o amigo. ¿Te sientes a salvo? Tómense de la mano cuando vayan a lugares, te ayudará a sentirte seguro y amado. Por la noche, "siente" la seguridad de estar arropado en tu cama.

¿Por qué tengo sueño?

Cada día damos nuestro mejor esfuerzo. Ahora tengo sueño y voy a descansar.

Pon tu mano cerca de tu boca y bosteza. ¿Te dio sueño? Da besos de buenas noches y cierra los ojos suavemente para dormir.

About the Author

Ken Stevens, born in Queens, N.Y., has published three previous works by Balboa Press, a division of Hay House, in the USA. His first book, "Your Creativity Unleashed" 1994, helps guide adult readers to a better way of life with 12 actionable chapters. He then created a new genre Spiritual Poetry Collection. His first poem book, "Loves Impressions" 1994, helped him heal his grief over the loss of his grandfather when he was only 16 years of age. His second poem book, "Revelations 111", 1995 is a culmination and curation of over 150 poems to 111 in total. It has 10 chapters of Virtue chakra-based, colorful pages with white text (the natural color of the paper}. A poem book to help a person to a achieve a better way of life. He enjoys book signings, having previously shared 5 Barnes and Nobles Events with interested readers.

About the Illustrator

Carmen Pacheco, born in Puerto Rico, is the President of <u>Conexbee.com</u>. This is her debut work, as an illustrator. Her talent as a graphic artist, shines through in her command of color, texture, and form. She has over 18 years of graphic design experience at agencies before venturing out on her own. She shares the love of creation and collaboration for success. She achieved her Bachelor of Arts degree in Puerto Rico before calling Orlando her home.

Printed in the United States
by Baker & Taylor Publisher Services